AF751582

AMAZING STRUCTURES

Amazing Modern Structures

CAROLINE THOMAS

REDBACK publishing

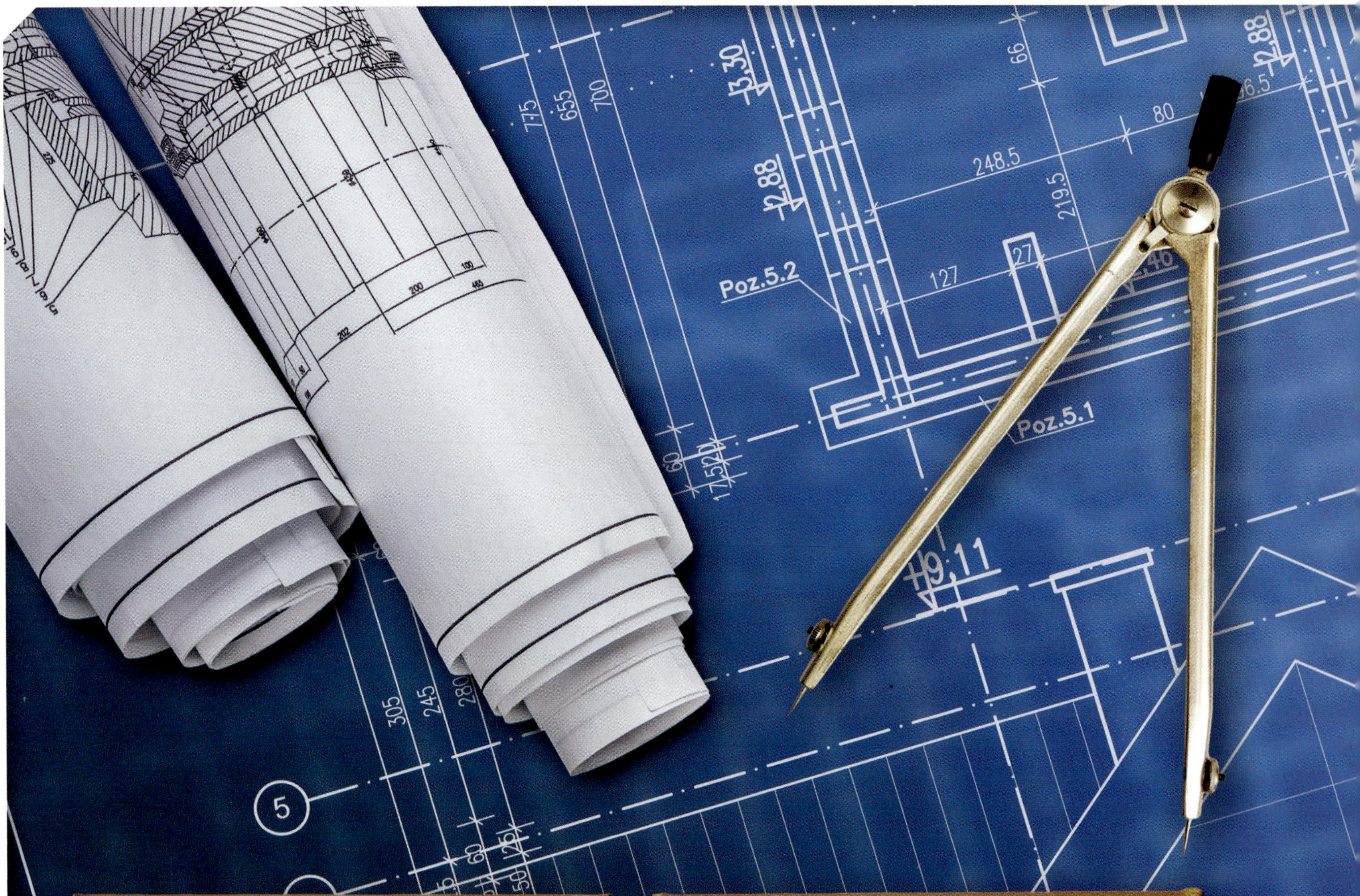

First Published
by Redback Publishing
PO Box 357 Frenchs Forest NSW 2086
Australia

www.redbackpublishing.com.au
orders@redbackpublishing.com.au

ISBN 978-1-76140-011-7 PBK

A catalogue record for this book is available from the National Library of Australia

Author: Caroline Thomas
Designer: Redback Publishing

Originated by Redback Publishing
Printed and bound in Malaysia

Every effort has been made to contact copyright holders of any material reproduced in this book. Any omissions will be rectified in subsequent printings if notice is given to the publisher.

Acknowledgements
Abbreviations: l–left, r–right, b–bottom, t–top, c–centre, m–middle
We would like to thank the following for permission to reproduce photographs: (Images © shutterstock), p4tr Valdis Skudre, p5tl, p14, p31tc Oliver Foerstner, p5tc, p20c Fitria Ramli, p5mc, p21c, p31bc Creative Family, p5bc, p10, p30tr In Green, p5rc, p24tl Weiming Xie, p5rb, p6b EQRoy, p6tl photo.ua, p30tl Chicago Architectural Photographing Company, Public domain, via Wikimedia Commons, p7c photo.ua, p8l, p30bmr Rahhal, p8ml Pavel L Photo and Video, p8mr kiraziku2u, p8r Fabio Nodari, p9l Yeti-Hunter, CC BY-SA 4.0 (https://creativecommons.org/licenses/by-sa/4.0), via Wikimedia Commons, p9ml KT Landscape image, p9cl IndustryAndTravel, p9cr そらみみ, CC BY-SA 4.0 (https://creativecommons.org/licenses/by-sa/4.0), via Wikimedia Commons, p9mr Heng Lim, p9r song jun, p11tc, p30bc MARIUSZ CZAJKOWSKI, p11b Claudio Divizia, p12, p31tml Pit Stock, p13 Mihir Ashar, p14 Oliver Foerstner, p15tc Warren Eisenberg, p15b HannaTor, p16tr Nick-D, CC BY-SA 4.0 (https://creativecommons.org/licenses/by-sa/4.0), via Wikimedia Commons, p16b, p31bl SAKARET, p17bl cornfield, p18c William Warby, CC BY 3.0 (https://creativecommons.org/licenses/by/3.0), via Wikimedia Commons, p18bl Felipe Gabaldón, CC BY 2.0 (https://creativecommons.org/licenses/by/2.0), via Wikimedia Commons, p19, p31br Mostak Ahmed, p20br Laura Peña, CC BY-SA 3.0 (https://creativecommons.org/licenses/by-sa/3.0), via Wikimedia Commons, p21tl Myroslava Bozhko, p22, p31bcl zhang wei9, p23l photo.ua, p23tr VOJTa Herout, p25tl Touseef designer, p28-p29 valeriy eydlin, p28tl Benny Marty, p28bl Mike Goad, Public domain, via Wikimedia Commons, p28br wantanddo, p29tr Michael Rieger, Public domain, via Wikimedia Commons, p29br Patrick Poendl, p30tc ArliftAtoz2205, p31tr PremChokli, p31bc Creative Family, p31bcr Hope Phillips

Contents

MODERN

Modern Landmarks Key

1. Empire State Building, USA
2. The Eiffel Tower, France
3. The Shard, England
4. CopenHill, Denmark
5. National Museum of Qatar, Qatar
6. Capital Gate, United Arab Emirates
7. Louvre Abu Dhabi, United Arab Emirates
8. Hong Kong-Zhuhai-Macau Bridge, China
9. Beijing Daxing International Airport, China
10. Sydney Opera House, Australia

All over the world, people have built structures, buildings and whole cities that can amaze and inspire. People travel far and wide to marvel at these incredible structures, admiring their beauty or innovation, as well as the manpower and tenacity it took to create them.

LANDMARKS

One Vision, Many Hands

Many of these structures were the vision of one person, but built by many. In modern times, **architects** and **engineers** are artists, using steel and **concrete** as their canvas. They create enormous works of art in cities all over the world.

GLOBAL

TRAILBLAZERS

Home Insurance Building, USA

Opened in 1885, Chicago's Home Insurance Building is considered to be the world's first **skyscraper**. Architect William Jenney developed a steel frame design after seeing his wife put a heavy book on top of a wire birdcage. He realised that the birdcage was stable because the weight was spread evenly through all of the wires. Jenney used this idea to revolutionise architecture and began the global race to build taller and taller structures. It was demolished in 1931 to make way for the LaSalle National Bank Building.

The Sydney Opera House, Australia

The Sydney Opera House is one of the most important public buildings in Australia and has been a **UNESCO World Heritage Site** since 2007. It is iconic in its design, use of original engineering methods and historic location. The Opera House sits on Bennelong Point, on the land of the Gadigal Aboriginal people.

In 2015, the Sydney Opera House became one of the few heritage buildings in the world to become certified as **Carbon Neutral**. Its interior is kept consistently cool by cold seawater from the harbour below, which circulates through 35 kilometres of internal piping to heat or cool the building. This saves 15 million litres of drinking water every year.

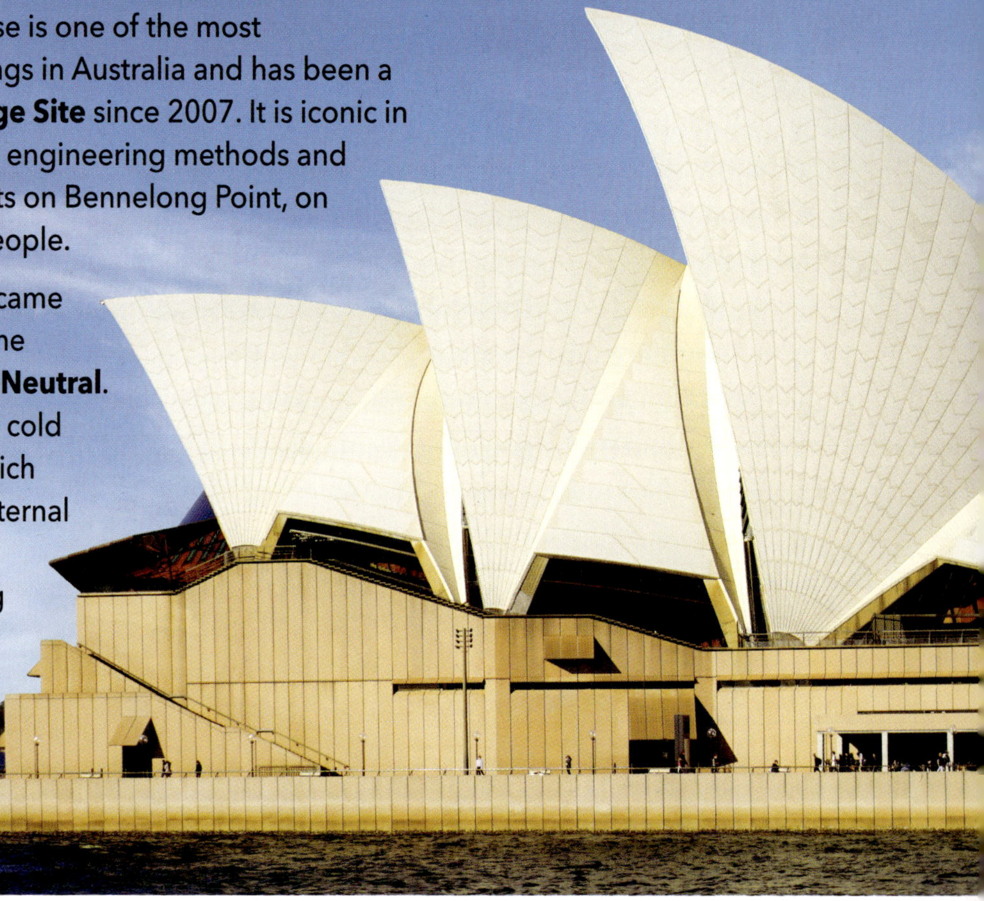

The Empire State Building, USA

Completed in 1931, the Empire State Building was the first building to exceed 100 floors. It rises 443 metres above New York City and remains one of the world's most iconic **skyscrapers.**

The Empire State Building was constructed at a time of great change in the building industry. Tools and materials were advancing, which made the construction process more efficient. Almost 3,400 workers built four and a half storeys every week and the entire building was completed in just 20 months.

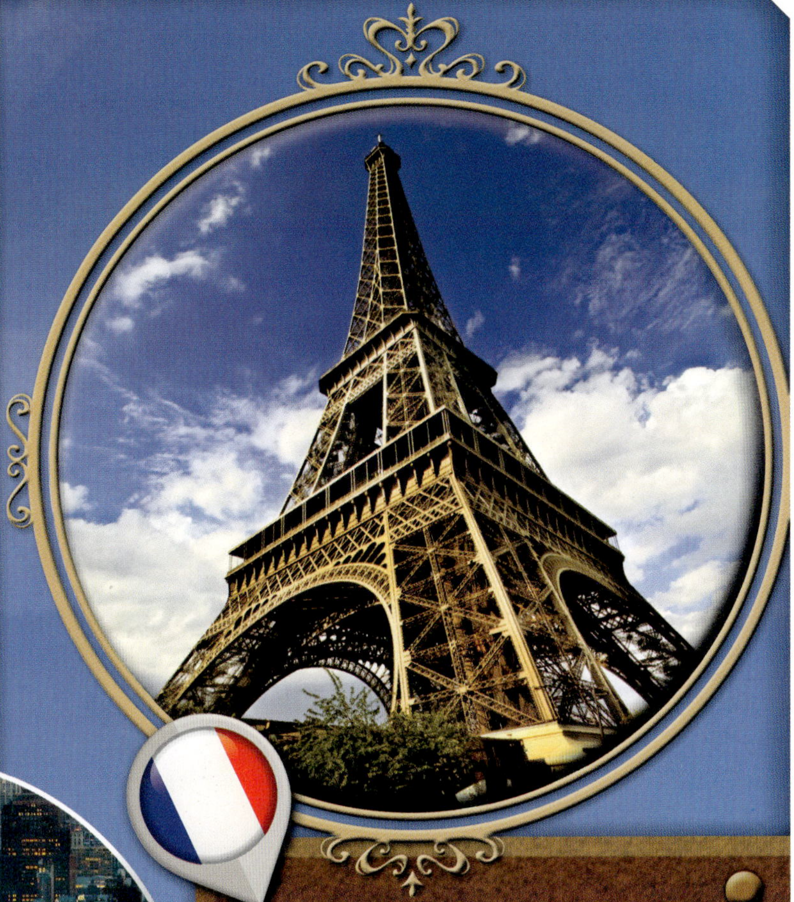

The Eiffel Tower, France

The Eiffel Tower is the most famous landmark in Paris and one of the most recognised structures in the world. It was built between 1887 and 1889 for the World Fair, marking the 100-year anniversary of the French Revolution. **Latticed** wrought iron was used to construct the tower, which was at that time both progressive and controversial. It was perfect for the tower's only purpose, which was to demonstrate French architectural creativity to the world.

The tower was intended to be removed after 20 years, but by then, Parisians could not bear to part with it and it now remains their most **iconic** landmark.

GLOBAL

SKYSCRAPERS

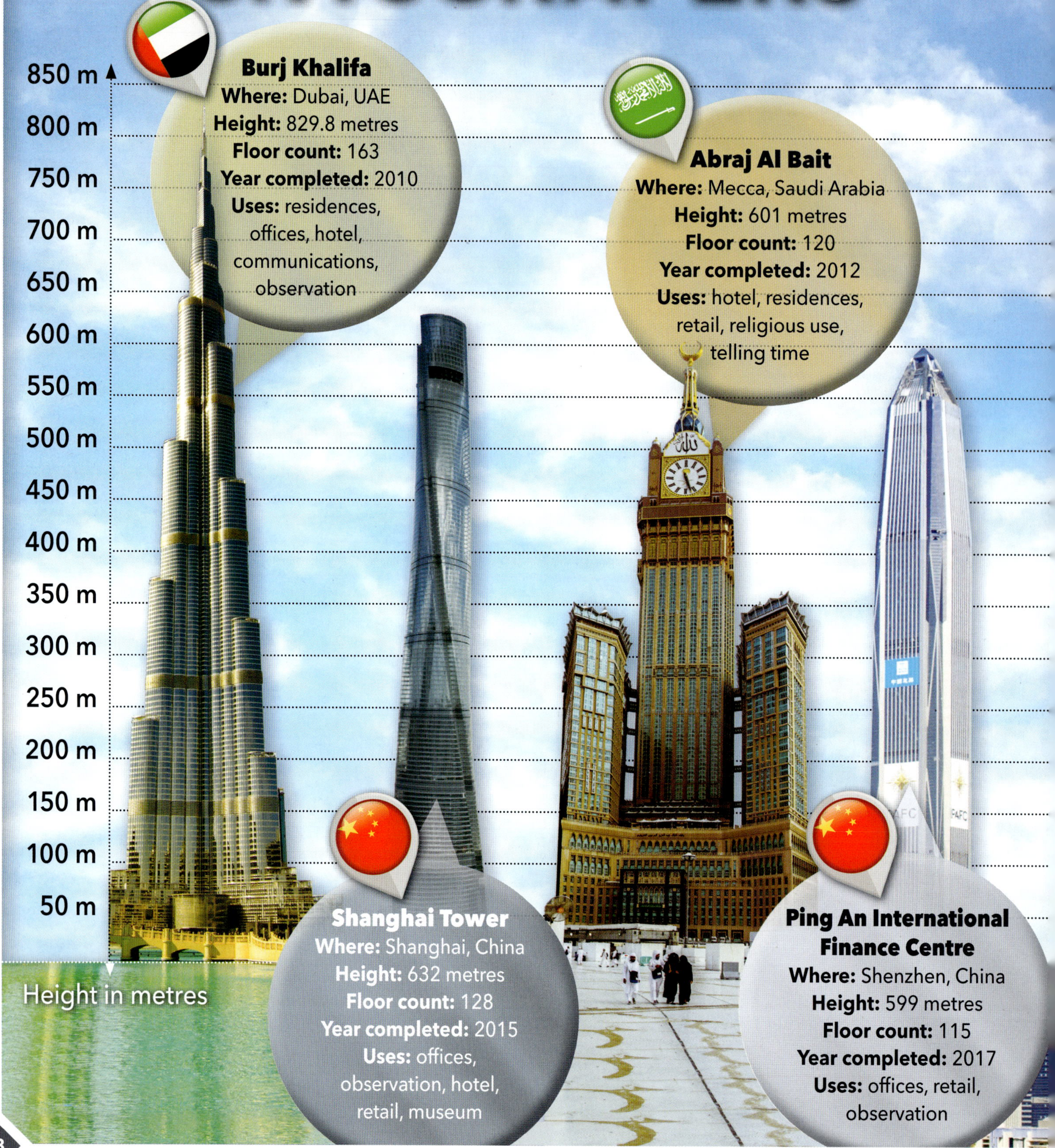

Burj Khalifa

Where: Dubai, UAE
Height: 829.8 metres
Floor count: 163
Year completed: 2010
Uses: residences, offices, hotel, communications, observation

Abraj Al Bait

Where: Mecca, Saudi Arabia
Height: 601 metres
Floor count: 120
Year completed: 2012
Uses: hotel, residences, retail, religious use, telling time

Shanghai Tower

Where: Shanghai, China
Height: 632 metres
Floor count: 128
Year completed: 2015
Uses: offices, observation, hotel, retail, museum

Ping An International Finance Centre

Where: Shenzhen, China
Height: 599 metres
Floor count: 115
Year completed: 2017
Uses: offices, retail, observation

City skylines around the world are now shaped by soaring skyscrapers. Since the 10-storey Home Insurance Building in Chicago was built in 1885, architects everywhere have tried to build taller and taller buildings.

The top 10 tallest buildings in 2022 are:

Goldin Finance 117
Where: Tianjin, China
Height: 597 metres
Floor count: 117
Year height achieved: 2019 (still under construction)
Uses: offices, hotel, residences, retail, observation

One World Trade Center
Where: New York City, USA
Height: 541 metres
Floor count: 104
Year completed: 2014
Uses: offices, observation, communications

Tianjin Chow Tai Fook Binhai Center
Where: Tianjin, China
Height: 530 metres
Floor count: 97
Year completed: 2019
Uses: offices, hotel, residences

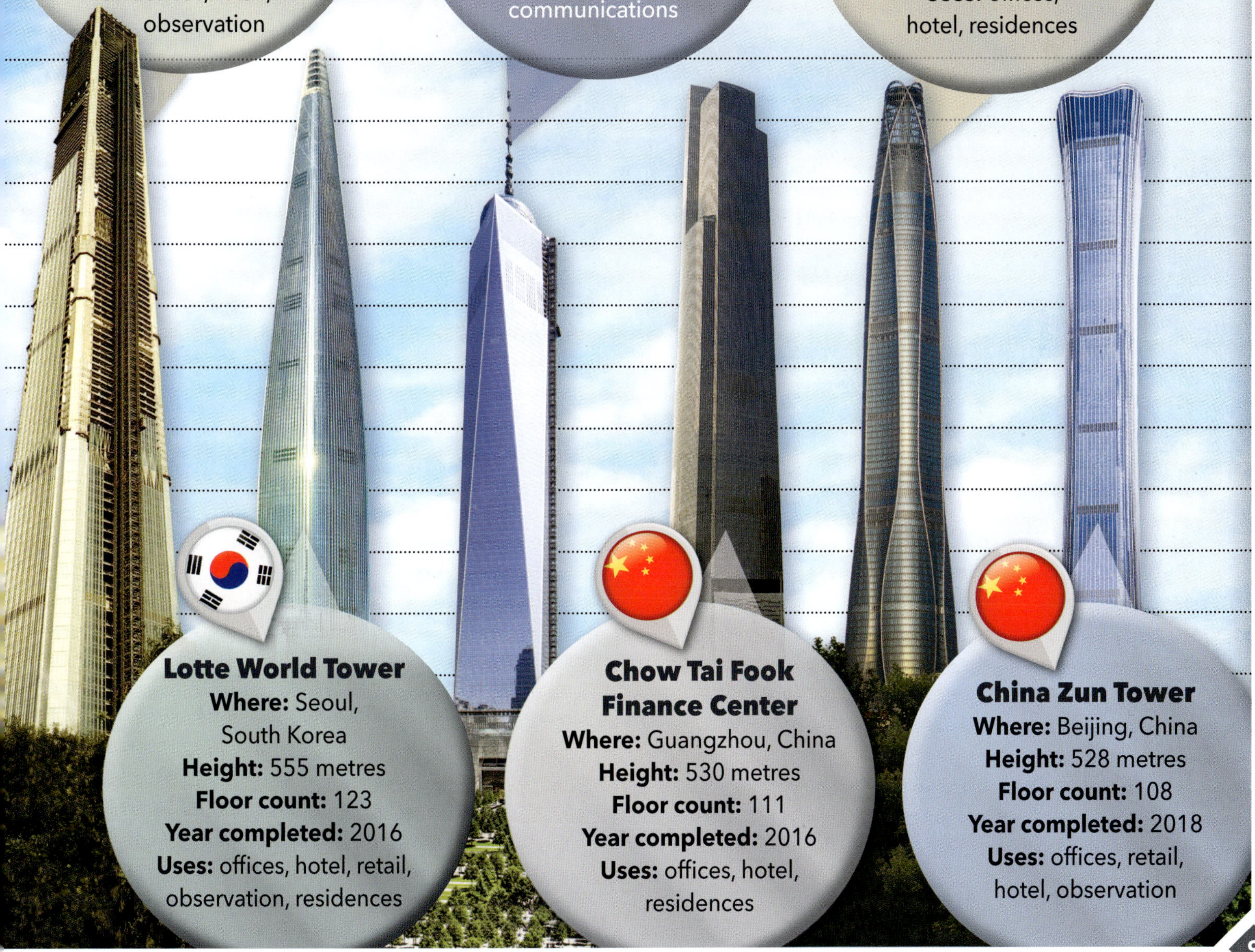

Lotte World Tower
Where: Seoul, South Korea
Height: 555 metres
Floor count: 123
Year completed: 2016
Uses: offices, hotel, retail, observation, residences

Chow Tai Fook Finance Center
Where: Guangzhou, China
Height: 530 metres
Floor count: 111
Year completed: 2016
Uses: offices, hotel, residences

China Zun Tower
Where: Beijing, China
Height: 528 metres
Floor count: 108
Year completed: 2018
Uses: offices, retail, hotel, observation

INSPIRED DESIGN

Capital Gate

Completed in 2011, Capital Gate is also known as the Leaning Tower of Abu Dhabi and is recognised by Guinness as the world's Farthest Man-made Leaning Building. This 160-metre tall tower leans 18 degrees to the west – almost five times the incline of the famous Leaning Tower of Pisa.

The tower is shaped like a funnel, widening as it reaches higher to make each of the internal spaces a different shape and size.

Core Strength

Engineers used 15,000 cubic metres of concrete, reinforced with 9 million kilograms of steel to build its core with a slight incline in the opposite direction to the final lean of the building.

It is further prevented from falling over by 490 one-metre wide concrete pilings that anchor its base 30 metres below the ground. In the harsh environment of Abu Dhabi, **wind resistance** and **seismic activity** make additional engineering essential.

The MI6 Building

The MI6 Building at Vauxhall Cross in London is the headquarters of the British Secret Intelligence Service. Officially opened by the Queen in 1994, the structure had to be specially designed as a fortress to protect the high level of foreign intelligence that was gathered and used within its walls. The building has multiple layers and 60 separate roof spaces.

The structure includes 12,000 square metres of 25 different types of glass and its many windows are triple glazed for added security. A large percentage of the building sits safely below ground and the building is surrounded by two moats for added security.

The MI6 building was designed by British architect Terry Farrell. It is nicknamed Babylon-On-Thames, because of its Aztec temple design.

GEOMETRIC DESIGN

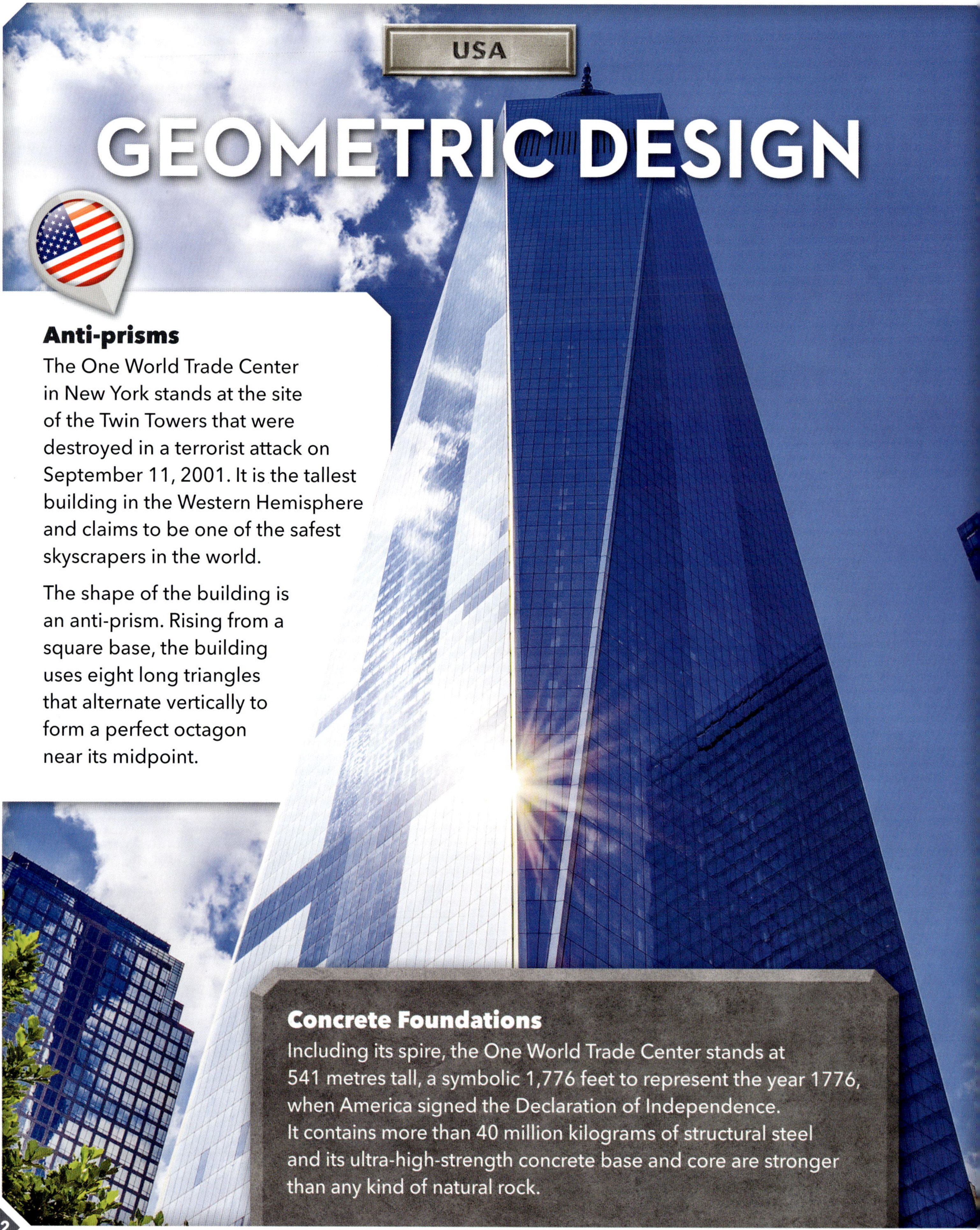

Anti-prisms

The One World Trade Center in New York stands at the site of the Twin Towers that were destroyed in a terrorist attack on September 11, 2001. It is the tallest building in the Western Hemisphere and claims to be one of the safest skyscrapers in the world.

The shape of the building is an anti-prism. Rising from a square base, the building uses eight long triangles that alternate vertically to form a perfect octagon near its midpoint.

Concrete Foundations

Including its spire, the One World Trade Center stands at 541 metres tall, a symbolic 1,776 feet to represent the year 1776, when America signed the Declaration of Independence. It contains more than 40 million kilograms of structural steel and its ultra-high-strength concrete base and core are stronger than any kind of natural rock.

UAE

Twisted Towers

Twisted towers are a growing trend in modern architecture. Dubai's Cayan Tower has 75 storeys and stands at 306 metres tall. It rotates a full 90 degrees from its base to its top, with each floor rotated 1.2 degrees more than the last, around a cylindrical elevator that acts like a spindle. The twisting shape works to reduce the amount of heat that can enter the building from the sun, as well as to deflect desert winds that can carry destructive fine sand particles.

Benefits With a Twist

Twisted designs work in three ways:

- They provide relief from the natural elements in harsh environments, to increase the efficiency of heating and cooling
- They better deflect wind resistance and so require less steel in their construction, meaning their construction costs much less
- They are more eye-catching and can change shape depending on the viewer's position

DENMARK

SUSTAINABLE DESIGN

CopenHill

CopenHill is the cleanest waste-to-energy plant in the world. It is also the most **aesthetically** pleasing and serves a dual purpose to its local residents, with Denmark's first-ever artificial ski slope on its roof. This has sparked global interest in city rooftops, which are now recognised as under-utilised yet valuable outdoor spaces. In urban areas, factory and office rooftops are now being re-evaluated for uses that can provide important recreational and outdoor spaces for their communities.

Up On the Roof

Urban rooftops make up approximately 25 percent of a city's total area. As new developments are designed, architects are now including better ways to make use of this extremely valuable space. Designs include urban farming, community parks, gardens, swimming pools and many other types of recreational space.

USA

The Shed

The Shed is an expandable exhibition hall in New York that can reduce its footprint depending on its needs. Used as a gallery and a performance space, this building has a telescopic shell that can respond to a variety of different artist's needs. Because it can be bigger or smaller, depending on the need at any given time, the carbon footprint of the building can be greatly reduced.

Roll With it

The canopy is 37 metres high when rolled out on its almost two-metre wide wheels. This creates a 56,000 cubic metre space that can hold up to 3,000 people. With synthetic pillows as the roof and walls, this temporary space can be temperature controlled much like a permanent structure.

This type of building design represents a shift towards more sustainable, temporary or adaptable structures that can serve a greater variety of uses while being environmentally conscious.

AUSTRALIA

One Central Park

Opened in 2013, One Central Park in Sydney, Australia is an apartment complex known for its rooftop gardens and hanging vertical gardens on its façade. In the basement is the world's largest water recycling plant in a residential building. Normal apartments return more than 90 percent of the water they consume straight into the sewer, but units in One Central Park return just three percent. Toilet flushing, washing machine use, irrigation, green-wall watering and air-cooling all use water that has been recycled on site.

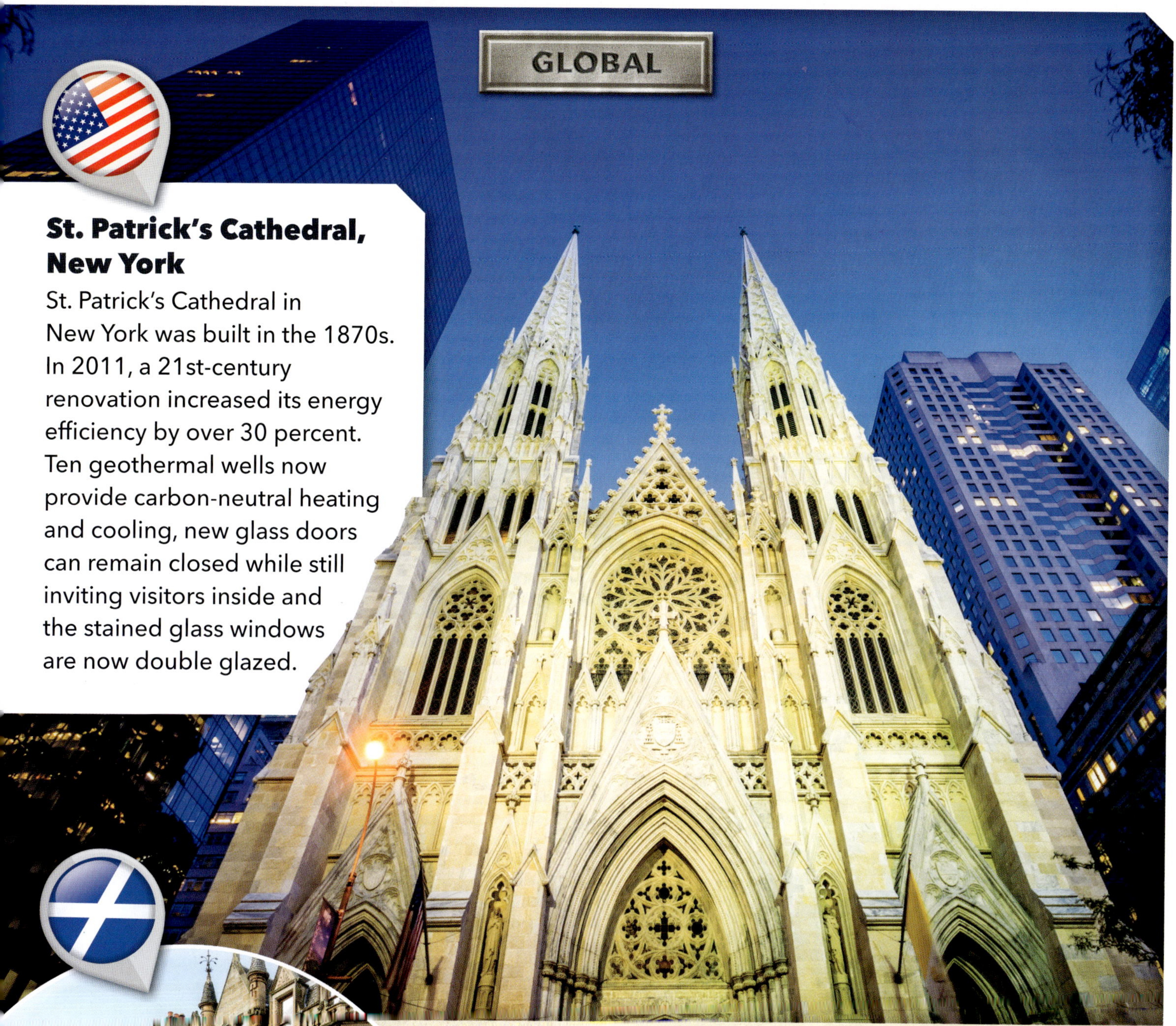

St. Patrick's Cathedral, New York

St. Patrick's Cathedral in New York was built in the 1870s. In 2011, a 21st-century renovation increased its energy efficiency by over 30 percent. Ten geothermal wells now provide carbon-neutral heating and cooling, new glass doors can remain closed while still inviting visitors inside and the stained glass windows are now double glazed.

Renovating for Sustainability

Sustainable design isn't only for new buildings. There are millions of historical homes and buildings around the world where retrofit, 21st-century renovation is extremely valuable. Many 19th and 20th-century buildings were built to last for hundreds of years but environmental efficiency was not a factor in their design.

In Glasgow, Scotland, some five-storey, sandstone tenement buildings date from the 1800s. Retrofits include insulation and non-fossil fuelled heating that can reduce their energy use by up to 90 percent.

SPAIN

VISUAL DESIGN

City of Arts and Sciences

The City of Arts and Sciences in Valencia, Spain, lies in what used to be the riverbed of the river Turia. The river was drained after a catastrophic flood in 1957, before being converted into a park. Construction began on the new City in 1996 and it was inaugurated in 1998.

Movie Magic

The city is a collection of **futuristic** buildings that include an opera house, Europe's largest aquarium, an IMAX cinema, a planetarium built in the shape of an eye, an interactive museum of science built in the shape of a whale skeleton, and an indigenous garden and sculpture park. The city has been used in several box office movies and high rating streaming series that feature futuristic buildings and cities.

Beijing Daxing International Airport

Beijing Daxing International Airport is the largest single-terminal airport in the world. It opened at the start of a global pandemic, in September 2019, with unprecedented global travel interruptions that continued for over two years. Despite this, almost 40 million passengers travelled through the terminal during that time.

Inspired by Nature

Designed to be as naturally lit and as compact as possible, the five aircraft piers are arranged around a central glass-domed terminal which creates the shape of a starfish. The construction took just four years to complete, with both materials and workers sourced only from those locally available.

FUTURISTIC DESIGN

National Museum of Qatar

Completed in 2019 and nicknamed the Desert Rose, Jean Nouvel's National Museum of Qatar creates a bridge between the past and the present. The building leads visitors on a 1.5-kilometre journey through a series of irregularly shaped and sized rooms, created from over 539 sand-coloured concrete discs in 30 different sizes.

Desert Rose

The disks are a representation of the desert rose crystal formations in the surrounding desert. They overhang the windows so that when the sun hits the building from the east or west, deep shadows keep the interior spaces cool. Inside the retail spaces of the museum, a 40,000-piece wooden puzzle transforms the ceilings into a Cave of Light.

Louvre Abu Dhabi

Built in 2017 and designed by Jean Nouvel, Abu Dhabi's Louvre is a museum city in the sea, accessible only by boat or pontoon. Its 55 individual buildings have ultra-high performance fibre concrete façades to help keep the internal temperature constant to protect the museum's artworks. A 180-metre diameter dome covers most of the buildings and is visible from the sea and the city.

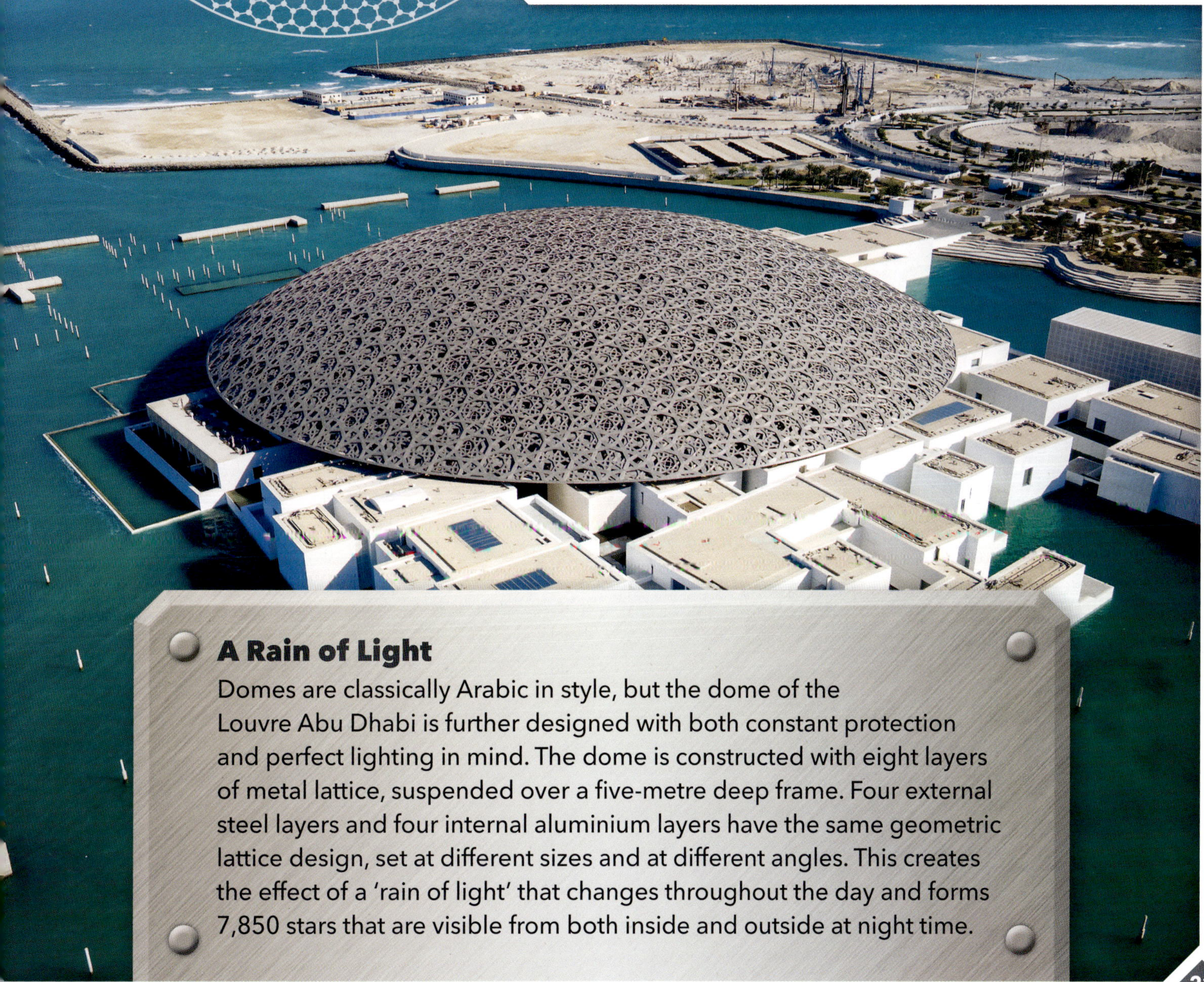

A Rain of Light

Domes are classically Arabic in style, but the dome of the Louvre Abu Dhabi is further designed with both constant protection and perfect lighting in mind. The dome is constructed with eight layers of metal lattice, suspended over a five-metre deep frame. Four external steel layers and four internal aluminium layers have the same geometric lattice design, set at different sizes and at different angles. This creates the effect of a 'rain of light' that changes throughout the day and forms 7,850 stars that are visible from both inside and outside at night time.

Sunrise Kempinski Hotel

Completed in 2014, the Sunrise Kempinski Hotel in Beijing is designed with Chinese symbolism in mind. It is as much a cultural statement as it is a functional hotel. Its shape as a rising sun symbolises China's growing economy, the fish mouth shape of the entrance symbolises prosperity, and the profile view of the building is meant to resemble a scallop, which represents 'fortune'.

The hotel stands at just 97 metres tall, but because it is located on the edge of Yanqi Lake, its reflection gives the appearance of a much larger building. The exposed, curved shape of the lantern-style exterior allows 25 percent more natural light through 10,000 glass panels. These panels are arranged so that the top portion of the building reflects the colour of the sky, the middle reflects the Yanshan Mountains and the bottom reflects the lake.

The Shard

London's, The Shard, was completed in 2012 and won first place at the Emporis Skyscraper Awards in 2014. It is the tallest building in Britain and its topmost 'shards' reach 306 metres high. It is designed to look like a shard of glass and uses 11,000 glass panels with a total area of 56,000 square metres.

30 St Mary Axe

30 St Mary Axe is an environmentally conscious skyscraper that uses its shape to increase natural lighting and **ventilation**. This reduces the building's energy consumption by over 50 percent. Spiralling light-wells naturally draw air upwards to ventilate the office interiors, while allowing natural daylight to shine right through the whole building.

MIGHTY BRIDGES

Hong Kong-Zhuhai-Macau Bridge

In October 2018, China opened the world's longest cross-sea bridge, connecting Hong Kong with Macau and the mainland's southern city of Zhuhai. At 55 kilometres long the bridge cuts the journey from Hong Kong to Zhuhai from four hours to just 30 minutes. Construction began in 2009 and included a 6.7-kilometre tunnel.

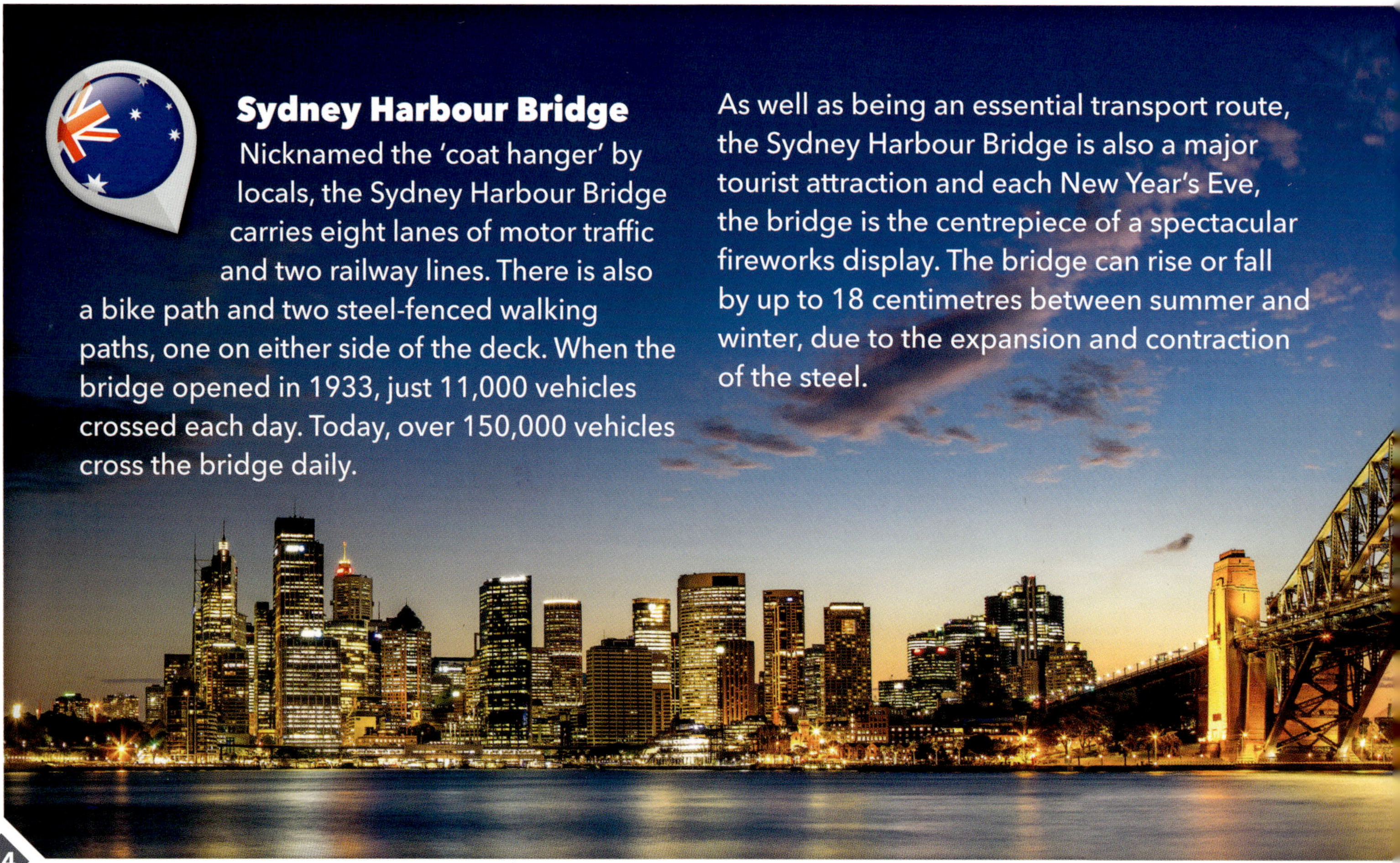

Sydney Harbour Bridge

Nicknamed the 'coat hanger' by locals, the Sydney Harbour Bridge carries eight lanes of motor traffic and two railway lines. There is also a bike path and two steel-fenced walking paths, one on either side of the deck. When the bridge opened in 1933, just 11,000 vehicles crossed each day. Today, over 150,000 vehicles cross the bridge daily.

As well as being an essential transport route, the Sydney Harbour Bridge is also a major tourist attraction and each New Year's Eve, the bridge is the centrepiece of a spectacular fireworks display. The bridge can rise or fall by up to 18 centimetres between summer and winter, due to the expansion and contraction of the steel.

Danyang-Kunshan Grand Bridge

The Danyang-Kunshan Grand Bridge in China is the longest bridge in the world. Designed and built to withstand typhoons, a magnitude-8 earthquake and a direct hit from a 270-million-kilogram naval vessel, the bridge is a marvel of modern engineering. It took four years and 10,000 workers to build the bridge, which stretches 164.8 kilometres from Shanghai to Nanjing.

GLOBAL

LIGHT OR AIR?

Light shines through the dome of the Louvre Abu Dhabi

Natural Light

To date, modern architecture has placed high importance on the **aesthetic** or 'look' of a building. This includes the visual experience of the people inside the building as well as the visual appeal from the outside. A huge part of this involved using as much natural light as possible and building spaces that include large portions of open-plan, shared and interconnected areas. Division of space has been seen as restrictive and unwanted, with many buildings even designed to blur the barrier between the outside and the inside.

High-density

High-density living has been seen as a way towards a healthier, more connected and supported society, with indoor spaces that are flooded with natural light becoming the new 'must-have'. Glass became the new brick, but not without consequence.

Main image: The skyline of Sydney's CBD

Fresh Air

Since the global pandemic that began in 2019, architects have begun to rethink the importance of light over fresh air. The problem with natural light is that large glass areas are expensive to engineer as functioning windows and cannot usually open. This has led to vast office complexes, hotels and apartment buildings where people have no functioning windows and no access to fresh air.

Changing Priorities

Light-filled city buildings rely on air conditioning, but this has now been shown to harbour and spread viruses. Open-plan working and living spaces mean that people cannot work or live in isolation if they need to and must share potentially infected air with others. This has led to a shift in thinking and new buildings are being designed, with a new focus in the wake of a pandemic. The way people use buildings to live and work is changing and designers must now solve the problem of providing fresh air within our city structures.

LEARNING FROM THE PAST

The Twin Towers in 1980

Events that changed the World

The coronavirus pandemic is not the first big event to change the way architects and engineers work. In 2001, when two hijacked planes purposely crashed into the twin towers of the World Trade Center in New York, no one – including its structural engineers – were prepared for what happened next.

Main image: "Tribute in Light' – a light installation that is projected annually on the anniversary of the September 11, 2001 attacks in memory of those lost

Weakened Structures

Where the planes hit the 110-storey building, those floors became engulfed in flames. This heated and weakened the structural steel of those floors and caused them to collapse, adding their load to the floor below. As each floor failed to hold the additional weight of the failed floors above, they too collapsed. It took about 10 seconds for the roofs of each of the 110-storey towers to hit the ground.

Progressive Solutions

Progressive collapse such as what happened that day is now much better understood and tall buildings have since been engineered to rely less on steel and more on ultra-high-strength concrete, that is not affected by heat.

The new One World Trade Center was completed in 2014

Modern STRUCTURES

1885
Home Insurance Building

1889
Eiffel Tower

1931
Empire State Building

1932
Sydney Harbour Bridge

1973
Sydney Opera House

1994
MI6 Building

1998 - 2009
City of Arts and Sciences

2010
Burj Khalifa

2011
Capital Gate

2012
The Shard

TIMELINE

2013
Cayan Tower

2013
One Central Park

2014
One World Trade Center

2014
Sunrise Kempinski

2017
Copenhill

2017
Louvre Abu Dhabi

2018
Hong Kong - Zhuhai-Macau Bridge

2019
National Museum of Qatar

2019
The Shed

2020
Beijing Daxing International Airport

Index

Glossary

aesthetics .... the way something looks

architect .... someone who designs a building

carbon neutral .... balanced emission of carbon and absorption of carbon

concrete .... blend of sand, cement, gravel and water used as a building material

engineer .... person who designs a building's structural elements to make it safe

foundation .... part of a building beneath ground-level that transfers weight to the earth

futuristic .... characteristic of an imagined future

iconic .... widely recognised

latticed .... regular geometrical arrangement that often looks criss-crossed

seismic activity .... relating to movement of the Earth due to volcanic activity

skyscraper .... building over 100 metres in height with multiple floors

UNESCO World Heritage Site .... site designated by the United Nations to be of worth to the world

ventilation .... purposeful introduction of outside air into an enclosed space

wind resistance .... effects of the forces of wind on a building